MW00928326

BIBLICAL PRINCIPLES FOR STARTING & OPERATING A BUSINESS

THE BIBLICAL ENTREPRENEURSHIP MARKETPLACE SERIES

Patrice Tsague

Edited by Esther Eyere, Michele Chatmon, Janice McMillian, Tyrone Grigsby and Shirley Powell.

Bloomington, IN Milton Keynes, UK

AuthorHouse™
1663 Liberty Drive, Suite 200
Bloomington, IN 47403
www.authorhouse.com
Phone: 1-800-839-8640

AuthorHouse™ UK Ltd.
500 Avebury Boulevard
Central Milton Keynes, MK9 2BE
www.authorhouse.co.uk
Phone: 08001974150

© 2006 Patrice Tsague. All rights reserved.

No part of this book may be reproduced, stored in a retrieval system, or transmitted by any means without the written permission of the author.

First published by AuthorHouse 10/12/2006

ISBN: 1-4259-4851-0 (sc)

Library of Congress Control Number: 2006906253

Printed in the United States of America
Bloomington, Indiana

This book is printed on acid-free paper.

Unless otherwise noted, Scripture quotations are taken from the King James Version, noted KJV Bible.

PRAISE FOR BIBLICAL PRINCIPLES FOR STARTING & OPERATING A BUSINESS

"There is only one correct way to do business; Gods way! Inspired by the Holy Spirit, this book speaks directly to the current needs of the Christian Entrepreneur. For everyone from the aspiring Sole Proprietor to the Fortune 500 CEO, if you want to learn what it takes to be a successful steward over your business this is a must read."

Derick W Hungerford
CEO, Residential Mortgage Corporation

"Here is a most remarkable young man who brought business to life for me. I first met Patrice Tsague and his wife Gina at a church sponsored program on managing your money. He shared his wilderness experience with money based on his upbringing. His mother had been the financial backbone of his family until he realized that he had to assume responsibility for his family and utilize the gifts and talents God had given him. My next encounter was the announcement of a biblically based business training program...a most intriguing concept to me. What has God got to do with business? It turned out to be the most fascinating, eye-opening experience I had ever had. I learned that my gifts and talents come from God and he expects me to use them to provide for the needs of his people (the entire world). It is the least that I can do for him. I have stewardship over the business. The business belongs to God and I am responsible to him to make a profit. It was overwhelming.

Nehemiah Project International is both a ministry and a business. God has used Patrice and Gina to do a good work in many of us who have benefited not only from the classes, but from his business coaching program as well. Now I run a successful business that serves the needs of the people in a way that glorifies the one who gave me the ability to do it. You can only grow in your understanding of God's plan for business by reading this book. There is no other option."

Jessica Haynes Franklin
CEO, Haynes Enterprises Consulting Services, Inc.

"At a time when the Holy Spirit is opening wide the doors for Christians to impact the global marketplace, Patrice Tsague's book on Biblical Entrepreneurship is a timely tool for the kingdom of God. Easy to read, this book combines sound biblical truths with relevant business principles, to equip readers desiring to become entrepreneurs with the information they need to succeed!"

Patricia Johnson, Associate Dean, Nyack College, Washington, DC
Author of "Journey Into God's Presence"

Biblical Entrepreneurship reminds us to follow the wisdom of God's Word and to exercise great diligence over the resources and abilities that our Lord entrusts to our care. I pray that all aspiring entrepreneurs will understand and act on Biblical precepts, to produce results in accordance with God's will for their lives.

Professor Jim Bechtel, Regent University School of Business

"Introduction to Biblical Entrepreneurship will lead you towards a better understanding of how you can be a part of God's economy, and will challenge you to rethink some of the most commonly accepted practices, values and purposes of business and our economic system! Every entrepreneur and businessperson should learn about Biblical Entrepreneurship."*

Doug Van Le
Executive Director, Eternal Words Spelling Bee
Promoting the Most Amazing Book!

<u>Dedication</u>

This book is dedicated to my three first ladies, my wife and best friend Gina and my two daughters Gabrielle and Danielle. Thank you for bearing with me and for loving me just as I am.

<u>Special Thanks</u>

Special thanks to all of those who have made my life, ministry and this book possible. I would like to thank my family, Biblical Entrepreneurs, my clients, my pastors, the NPIM family, our financial supporters, the From the Heart Church family and my present church family at Bethel World Outreach Ministries. I love you all.

Table of Contents

Foreward

By Tyrone Grigsby

Why are so many businesses that are owned and operated by Christians so indistinguishable from non-Christian businesses? Why are the quality of goods and services provided, in many instances, worse than those provided by non-Christian businesses? Why are Christians not setting the standards for business throughout the world? I believe the answer is simply a lack of knowledge. That is, a lack of knowledge of business administration principles and practices and, more importantly, a lack of knowledge of the biblical principles and practices set forth in the bible. Many Christian business people tend to lean to their own understanding and follow worldly business practices. Therefore, many of our Christian businesses are struggling, if not failing, both spiritually and naturally in the conduct of their business operations. What poor witnesses for the Lord.

Early in my Christian walk, a Christian businessman said to me, "I don't believe you can operate a business by the Word of God." With my very limited knowledge of the Scriptures, I did not then believe that statement to be true and am now fully persuaded that it is not true.

The Scriptures have much to say about how Christians are to operate businesses. Christian business persons are an essential part of God's plan for reconciling people to Christ. For instance, we have a major advantage that non-Christians do not have. The Lord tells us in Deuteronomy 8:18, *"But thou shalt remember the Lord thy God: for it is He that giveth thee <u>power to get wealth</u>, that He may establish His covenant ..."* Biblical Entrepreneurs must understand and appreciate the advantages we have as Christians because He gives us this power. In this present dispensation, much of that power resides in our relationship with the Holy Spirit of God. We must understand how to access that power in order to prosper according to God's will for our lives.

Christian businesses need more than instruction in the traditional functions of marketing, finance, administration and operations. They also need instruction in the principles of God as they apply to these functions and other aspects of entrepreneurship. Unfortunately, many Christian businesses have not been exposed to biblically based teachings that provide them with the sufficient and practical knowledge of God's word that is needed to make the connection between their businesses, all other aspects of their lives and the individual plan of God for their lives. Most pastors, preachers, evangelists and other teachers of the Word of God emphasize our relationships with and between God, family, church, community, other believers and non-believers. Many of these teachers do an excellent job of teaching these areas of Scripture; all of which are necessary. However, there is a lack of teaching from the pulpit about the subject of Biblical Entrepreneurship. Because of this lack of knowledge, Christian businesspersons are operating in a self-imposed bondage, not having the necessary information to make godly decisions. The bible tells us in II Corinthians

5:18, 20 *"And all things are of God, who hath reconciled us to Himself by Jesus Christ, and hath given to us the ministry of reconciliation. Now then we are ambassadors for Christ ...."* Here the Scriptures tell us that we are representatives of Christ in the earth and that He has given us the ministry to seek and save the lost. In other words, everyone who has accepted Jesus Christ as their Lord and Savior is a part of this ministry. The question that arises here is, how do I exercise my role as ambassador for Jesus Christ in the conduct of my business affairs? How am I to reconcile others to Christ while operating a business?

Successful Christian business people have the opportunity to influence the lives of many people: employees, suppliers, business associates, family and friends, community leaders, governmental officials, and others. Successful business people can have a significant impact upon the laws, policies and procedures in our communities. Their sphere of influence tend to be larger than most. They have the ability to reach a lot of people. Therefore, it is of great importance for Christian business people to be the most credible witnesses possible in these spheres of influence. In such perilous times as we now live in, we want the world to seek us out for answers to conditions and situations in our communities and around the world. We want non-believers to have what we have (salvation and a relationship with Jesus Christ). We want current and aspiring Christian business owners to have the knowledge they need to grow in their relationship with the Lord as their businesses grow and prosper.

Through the ministry of Nehemiah Project International Ministries, Inc., many current and aspiring business people, to their surprise, have developed a much closer relationship with the Lord. Many of the testimonies we receive are more about their established and/or improved relationship with Jesus Christ that results from specific study and focus on what God has to say, and expects from His people who are called to entrepreneurship. Biblical Entrepreneurship instruction for youth provides our youth with an early and strong foundation for the development of their entrepreneurial interests.

As Biblical Entrepreneurs, we are required to assess situations and make responsible judgments for which we are accountable to God. This reality should heighten our resolve to seek God's help in becoming holy and righteous so that our business practices can more perfectly reflect His will.

Damascus Road Experience

The Story of How My Wife and I Became Biblical Entrepreneurs

"And he said unto me, My grace is sufficient for thee: for my strength is made perfect in weakness. Most gladly therefore will I rather glory in my infirmities, that the power of Christ may rest upon me" (II Corinthians 12:9).

ARRIVAL IN THE US

In 1983, two families, unbeknownst to each other and separated by thousands of miles of ocean, shared a vision for their children. That vision was to provide a better future for those children, ages 11 and 12, by sending them to the United States of America. So it was that I, Patrice Tsague, and the little girl who would grow up to become my wife, Gina Dorceus, arrived in the United States. God's hand was orchestrating our lives from the very start.

It was the desire of my mother and grandmother that I be educated in the United States, and then return to my birthplace of Cameroon, Central Africa, to assist my mother in operating her various businesses. Similarly, Gina's parents believed that America would provide greater opportunity for their daughter, and so Mrs. Dorceus, who had already moved to the United States, sent for her from Port-au-Prince, Haiti. That year, 1983, we both immigrated to the United States.

Gina and I attended school in the Washington, D.C. area, later graduating from Blair High School and Takoma Academy, respectively. We finally met one another as high school juniors while working at the Washington Adventist Hospital in Takoma Park, Maryland, and soon became best friends. After graduation, Gina went on to obtain her Associate Degree in Business Administration from Montgomery College. I was attending Montgomery College as well, but was forced to drop out after one semester. During this time, my country, Cameroon experienced civil unrest, which greatly affected my family. My mother, Mrs. Foning Francoise, was a member of Parliament and an avid supporter of the President of Cameroon at that time. Consequently, she was targeted by those who wanted to remove the president from power. Her businesses and homes were destroyed, and she was no longer able to support me financially. As a young man in the United States, I had been living a carefree life without personal responsibility. Circumstances forced me to take matters into my own hands and to seek to build a life for myself. I didn't know it at the time, but it was the beginning of my pre-salvation wilderness experience. The process had begun through which God would draw me to Himself, humble me, prepare and perfect me to fulfill His purpose for my life.

THE DAYS OF EGYPT: "PRE-SALVATION WILDERNESS EXPERIENCE"

I had been coasting in my job at Washington Adventist, but once I realized that I could not continue college without earning enough money to pay for college myself, I began earnestly to seek a raise and promotion at work. After a year of trying, I finally received a raise...of ten cents. I then attempted to transfer to any higher-paid department, but to no avail. Stuck in the same place, I sought help from the director of Human Resources about my need but I had no success - only promises. Frustrated by all this, I began to look within myself...what was it that I was passionate about? What could I apply myself to, what did I enjoy? What was it that I could do, and have a greater chance of achieving long-term success? I began to pay closer attention to the people I worked with at the hospital. There were many who had been there for 10 or 15 years, even more. None seemed to be happy with their jobs, and none were economically free. I then made a decision that would change my life. I decided not to follow the example of so many around so that I don't find myself still unhappy and in bondage to this job ten years later.

After much reflection I realized that from my youth up, I had always wanted to start a business, and to help others. This passion was greatly influenced by my mother's example. In Cameroon she had operated several businesses: a construction company, an import/export company, a restaurant, a college, a clinic, and many others while at the same time serving as both a humanitarian and a politician. She employed over 1000 people at one time, sent hundreds of young people to Europe and the United States, paid for children's education, helped families and financed her own political campaigns. Growing up in the midst of all this created in me a desire to own a business so I could enjoy the same freedom and ability to impact the lives of others. Once I came to this realization, I called my mother and requested permission to delay college and start a business, which she granted. This led me into years of personal challenges and difficulties as I was searching for who I was and what I was on this earth for. I slept in my car, on stairways of apartment buildings, on the floor of Gina's house, in my office. There were days when I wanted to give up, but what kept me going was reflecting upon my mother's own journey and the companionship that Gina provided me.

THE JOURNEY TO ENTREPRENEURSHIP

Now that I had determined that entrepreneurship was the answer, I thought maybe an import/export business would be the way to go, since my family was already involved in that industry. I thought that I could import goods from Cameroon and export items back from the United States, tapping into the family business infrastructure to get started. I did just that, with my business indeed serving as the family's American base. However, the business was short lived because I soon learned that I did not share the same business philosophy as my brothers and sisters. I then decided to start completely from scratch, and over a delicious Popeye's Chicken meal, I shared my business idea with Gina and invited her to join me as my partner. The idea I shared was a company which we would call PG Enterprises. PG Enterprises would join several network marketing companies (starting with Mary Kay), and build a marketing company that would create opportunities for others in various industries. Gina would head the Mary Kay department. She agreed and PG Enterprises was born.

Despite her concerns about my dropping out of school, my aunt gave me $500.00 to invest in the business. As Gina and I began to share our business concept with others, and recruit a team of people to work with us, I soon realized that I had a greater passion to see others grow than to build a business for myself. We followed that passion, and the transition began. The focus of PG Enterprises changed from that of building for profit businesses to establishing a non-profit organization that would help others start their own business. That non-profit organization was christened the Multi-Cultural Youth Educational Organization Incorporated, or MCY.

THE BIRTH OF MCY

In May of 1993, MCY was organized to provide leadership and entrepreneurship training, business planning workshops and seminars and financing for youth and young adults. MCY served over 300 teens and young adults in the Washington Metropolitan area. We also worked with several organizations in the area, including the National Foundation for Teaching Entrepreneurship, the Washington Urban League, the Baltimore Opportunity Industrial Center, and the Small Business Administration District Office, to name a few.

As MCY was a non-profit organization, fund-raising was in itself a full-time job. During a conference in which I hoped to garner more sponsors to support the organization, I was introduced to a businessman named Tyrone Grigsby. Mr. Grigsby was the founder of a company called Network Solutions. He was also known in our circle as the $40 million dollar man; his company was named one of Black Enterprise Magazine's 100 most profitable businesses. The MCY Chairman of the Board, Larry Bland, recommended that I speak with Mr. Grigsby about supporting our work. As I shared with him what we were doing, he took great interest and committed to mentoring me and helping us to achieve our mission. He was particularly moved by the fact that we were committed to teaching our youth how to achieve success both legally and morally. Mr. Grigsby, a committed Christian, began to meet regularly with me, mentoring and sharing the Gospel of Jesus Christ. Two books that he gave me during this time changed my life. The books were The Richest Man in Babylon, and the African American Heritage Bible. He also gave me many tapes of messages given by Dr. Myles Munroe, and by the pastor of his church, John A. Cherry.

SALVATION

In December, 1994, Mr. Grigsby invited me to attend a men's retreat with him. Thinking we were going to a businessmen's retreat, I packed my sports gear and prepared myself for golfing, swimming and other recreational activities. I was certain that this retreat would teach me how to grow the organization, and provide excellent networking opportunities. As we arrived at the retreat site, I soon realized that it was a Christian men's retreat that had been organized by Mr. Grigsby's church, Full Gospel A.M.E. Zion Church (now From the Heart Church Ministries). One of the guest ministers, Pastor Ira Hilliard from Dallas, Texas, conducted the service the first night. As he preached, I heard the Gospel like I had never heard before. It seemed as though Pastor Hilliard was preaching my entire life story. Moved by the Spirit and convicted by the message, I accepted Jesus Christ as my Lord and Savior that night and later joined Full Gospel. When I got back from the retreat, I excitedly shared all that happened with Gina. She began to see a change in me, and those changes caused her to want that same Jesus who had so changed my life. Gina accepted Christ's free gift of salvation, and joined me as a member of Full Gospel. A year later, on December 5, 1995, Gina and I got married.

CALL INTO THE MINISTRY

The first retreat I attended saved my soul, but the second retreat was where I began to surrender to the Lordship of Jesus Christ. My perspective on everything changed, especially concerning the work we were doing at MCY. Gina and I both realized that with all the good that was happening through our organization, if the youth did not leave us knowing Jesus Christ as Savior and Lord, all of our work was for naught. At the next men's retreat, I heard and responded to God's call to Christian ministry. I had only been a Christian for a year, and struggled with the idea of a "call." What exactly did that mean? As I wrestled with that question, a statement made by my pastor, John A. Cherry, provided me with some direction. He said "When you don't know what to do, do what you know now to do." What I knew was entrepreneurship. As a result, our mission at MCY changed. We began the transition from a secular to a Christian training organization. As I continued in what I knew, and followed the instructions of God, He revealed my call to use entrepreneurship as a tool to empower the Body of Christ and lead the lost to a saving knowledge of Jesus Christ.

THE BIRTH OF BIBLICAL ENTREPRENEURSHIP (BE)

In December of 1996, at yet another Full Gospel Men's Retreat, the Lord inspired me to develop a biblically based curriculum to teach entrepreneurship to teens and adults. By the grace of God, with the assistance of Mr. Grigsby and Pastor Cherry's teachings, Gina and I began developing the Biblical Entrepreneurship curriculum. Some months later, the first Biblical Entrepreneurship (BE) class began with seven registered students. Two years later MCY sponsored five classes with a total of 47 program participants. With the financial support of Mr. Grigsby, MCY opened a Biblical Entrepreneurship Training Center in Silver Spring, Maryland. In addition, a Mustard Seed Grant Award enabled MCY to launch a Micro Loan Program to provide seed capital to its graduates. In 1998, the Lord led us to bring the entire Biblical Entrepreneurship program under the covering of, and into operation in Full Gospel A.M.E. Zion Church.

THE BIRTH OF NPIM

In November, 1998, my mother visited us in the US. She was inspired by what the Lord was doing in our lives, and in the life of MCY. She invited us to visit the family home in Cameroon, Central Africa. Believing this was all part of God's plan for us, Gina and I sought direction from the Lord as to how we could glorify Him in our visit. We were led to meet with Bishop Darlingston Johnson, Pastor of Bethel World Outreach Church of Silver Spring, Maryland. During our meeting with Bishop Johnson, we were introduced to Pastor Charles K. Wesley, of Bethel World Outreach Church Ministries in Douala, Cameroon. Through the meeting with Pastor Wesley and one of his associates, Gina and I learned about the miserable spiritual and economic conditions that existed in Cameroon. Pastor Wesley encouraged us to bring our ministry to Africa in hopes of addressing the desperate need for economic empowerment of God's people there. The Lord gave us a vision from the book of Nehemiah, and thus 'The Nehemiah Project' was born. Initially, we envisioned the Nehemiah Project as a potential program within MCY through which resources such as computer products could be sent to Cameroon. During our three-week stay in

Cameroon, not only was the need for the vision confirmed, but the full vision of the Nehemiah Project was revealed. What we thought would be a program sponsored by MCY became the Nehemiah Project International Ministries (NPIM). While in Cameroon, my wife and I taught a series of Bible studies, held prayer sessions, donated over 70 French Bibles and led numerous people to the saving knowledge of the Lord Jesus Christ.

Bethel World Outreach Church in Douala and Living Word Missions were the first to embrace the NPIM vision. The Lord opened doors everywhere. A Christian lawyer volunteered her services to help draft the legal papers for the Nehemiah Project Chapter of Cameroon. A covenant partnership was established with Bethel World Outreach Church in Douala, Living Word Missions, and my mother, Mrs. Francoise, businesswoman and governmental representative in Cameroon. Upon our return to the United States, our new direction was confirmed through a teaching by Pastor Cherry entitled "Allow God to Do a New Thing" taken from Isaiah 43:10. My wife and I developed a plan to transition from MCY to Nehemiah beginning with the closing of the training center. We began to offer Biblical Entrepreneurship Training classes through local churches; St. Paul Church and From the Heart Church Ministries (formerly Full Gospel) were the first. The MCY family offered their full support and on May 25, 1999, MCY's Articles of Incorporation were amended to officially change the name and mission of the organization. Nehemiah Project International Ministries Incorporated was officially born. This was the biggest leap of faith yet, as we had to forsake secular resources and trust in God's faithfulness to give us direction and provision. God has been true to His Word. We have faced many challenges and many times we have felt inadequate to do the great work He has given us to do. But time after time, the Lord has shown us that His strength is made perfect in weakness as we continue in His calling for our lives.

Today, the Nehemiah Project International Ministries works in partnership with local churches, Christian educational organizations and businesses in the United States, and in other parts of the world. We provide biblically based entrepreneurship education and business support services to individuals in business and those seeking to start and operate a business. Our mission is to help people fulfill God's plan for their lives through business. Our courses are offered through local churches, Christian universities, community organizations as well as through a state of the art online campus. Individuals who complete our courses are eligible to become members of the Biblical Entrepreneurship Alumni Association (BEAA) where they receive support in the growth and development of their businesses while being encouraged to contribute to the advancement of God's kingdom in their communities and throughout the world.

1

12 Principles of God's Economy (Based on Matthew 25:14-46)

"For the kingdom of heaven is as a man travelling into a far country, who called his own servants, and delivered unto them his goods" (Matthew 25:14).

In Matthew 25:14-30, our Lord and Savior Jesus Christ compares the kingdom of heaven with a man who gave his servants goods to maintain while he traveled to a faraway land. The master in this parable represents the Lord Jesus and the servants represent us, His servants. The goods, or talents, represent the gifts, skills and treasures God has given each of us according to our individual abilities. Ability is the power and strength granted to you by God that enables you to use your gifts, skills and treasures to His glory.

As the story progresses, the servant with five talents trades his talents and gains five more, while the one given two talents trades his talents and gains an additional two. The servant who was given one talent fearfully buries his under ground. Upon his return, the master asks the servants to give a report on what they have done with the talents he gave them. The first servant reports, *"Lord, thou deliveredst unto me five talents: behold, I have gained beside them five talents more"* (Matthew 25:20). The second servant says, *"Lord, thou deliveredst unto me two talents: behold, I have gained two other talents beside them"* (Matthew

25:22). To these two servants, the master says *"Well done, thou good and faithful servant: thou hast been faithful over a few things, I will make thee ruler over many things: enter thou into the joy of thy lord"* (Matthew 25:23).

Finally the third servant, who received one talent, gives an account of his stewardship: *"Lord, I knew thee that thou art an hard man, reaping where thou hast not sown, and gathering where thou hast not strawed: And I was afraid, and went and hid thy talent in the earth: lo, there thou hast that is thine"* (Matthew 25:24-25). The master responds by saying, *"Thou wicked and slothful servant, thou knewest that I reap where I sowed not, and gather where I have not strawed: Thou oughtest therefore to have put my money to the exchangers, and then at my coming I should have received mine own with usury. Take therefore the talent from him, and give it unto him which hath ten talents. For unto every one that hath shall be given, and he shall have abundance: but from him that hath not shall be taken even that which he hath"* (Matthew 25:26-29). The master then casts the unprofitable servant into outer darkness.

Just like the three servants in the story, your Master, the Lord Jesus Christ, has given you "talents." These talents are in the form of gifts, skills and treasures. Gifts are God's spiritual blessings upon you, by the operation of the Holy Spirit, to fulfill a divine purpose. A skill is a God-given, natural trade, technique or special expertise requiring the use of the hand, body, or mind. Treasures are wealth in the form of valuables or money. God gave you these talents based on your ability to use them profitably. Have you identified your talents? Have you been using them profitably? Just as in the story of the talents, the Lord Jesus will be coming back to ask what you have done with your gifts, skills and treasures. From the parable of the talents we can find 12 biblical economic principles that will help us to effectively use our talents through business. Understanding how these economic principles work is crucial to doing business successfully from God's perspective. The principles are as follows:

1. God has given each of us talents in the form of gifts, skills and treasures based on our abilities.

These talents are also known in the business world as assets. An asset is something of value that can be used to generate a profit. Assets are essential to starting a business; they are that which God has given us to trade. Every child of God has assets, and these assets are given based on our abilities. Therefore, jealousy, envy and comparison have no place in our lives concerning assets and abilities. All that we have was given to us by the Lord based on His plan and purpose for our lives, not due to any great thing we have done. We must also guard against complacency, for God knows what ability He has given each of us. We will be judged by the stewardship we exercise over the assets and abilities with which we have been entrusted.

"For the kingdom of heaven is as a man traveling into a far country, who called his own servants, and delivered unto them his goods" (Matthew 25:14).

> **Assets = gifts + skills + treasures**

"And unto one he gave five talents, to another two, and to another one; to every man according to his several ability; and straightway took his journey" (Matthew 25:15).

2. **We each have a responsibility to exercise wise stewardship over our talents through trade.**

> **"You cannot start a business without an asset."**

Responsibility in this context means to be faithful in that which we have stewardship over. Stewardship is caring for the things (assets) of another. Whether or not you start a business, God requires you to make proper use of your talents or assets.

"Then he that had received the five talents went and traded with the same, and made them other five talents. And likewise he that had received two, he also gained other two" (Matthew 25:16-17).

3. Whenever there is trade, there must be a profit.

"Then he that had received the five talents went and traded with the same, and made them other five talents. And likewise he that had received two, he also gained other two" (Matthew 25:16-17).

> **"Whether you start a business or not, God requires you to make proper use of your talents or assets."**

To trade is to exchange something of value with an expectation of a higher return; it is to do business or to be productive. When we are productive, our work yields a profit. Unfortunately, many of us work without considering whether or not we are yielding a profit; the main concern is getting paid. Ask yourself the question, when I leave my workplace, have I left it in a better state than when I arrived? If not, then I have not been profitable in my workplace; my stewardship can justifiably be called into question. Profit is the tangible demonstration of my stewardship. God expects us, whether or not we start a business, to appreciate, or grow, the value of whatever He puts under our care. That is the goal of a steward, to appreciate the value of those things for which he is responsible. If you purchase a car, your stewardship of that car can be demonstrated by its resale value. Though cars inevitably depreciate in value, the better care you take of them, the higher your resale value will be. Consequently, when we trade the assets God has entrusted to us, God expects us to appreciate, or multiply them by our good stewardship.

4.   Profit is the fruit of proper stewardship and not the reward.

> **"The goal of the steward is to appreciate the value of the things he is responsible for."**

"And so he that had received five talents came and brought other five talents, saying, Lord, thou deliveredst unto me five talents: behold, I have gained beside them five talents more. He also that had received two talents came and said, Lord, thou deliveredst unto me two talents: behold, I have gained two other talents beside them" (Matthew 25:20,22).

Many business schools and consultants believe and teach that the goal of the entrepreneur is to make a profit and increase his standard of living; this is the reward of being a good entrepreneur. In Biblical Entrepreneurship, the business profit is not your reward for being a good entrepreneur or a good steward. Remember our first point; the assets that you start this business with are not yours. The gifts, skills and treasures are not yours; they are the Master's who has entrusted them to your care until He returns. For example, suppose you are a money manager and I gave you $25,000 to care for. Ten years later, I return to you for my investment. Based on your good stewardship, you increased it from $25,000 to $200,000. How much money do you owe me? $25,000 or $200,000? Of course the answer is $200,000, because the $25,000 you began with was not yours and neither is the increase of $175,000. The assets you began with belong to your Master and the increase of the assets is His as well; nothing belongs to you. So what does one do with the profit? The profit is used for the following three things:

I. **To reinvest in the business** – many entrepreneurs get so focused on enhancing their standard of living that they miss the fact that you must continuously reinvest in the business in order to increase the capacity of that business to produce, thereby serving more people. This should be the goal of every business.

II. **Enhance your products and services** – The sad reality is that many entrepreneurs begin with great products and services, but instead of improving those products and services over time, they look for ways to cut costs in order to make more money. Don't get me wrong, you should always look for more affordable ways to produce and deliver your goods, but never at the expense of quality. I am sure you can think of many products or services that have decreased in quality over time.

III. **To fulfill God's covenant** – Deuteronomy 8:18 tells us that God has given us power so that we may gain wealth to fulfill His covenant. We will go into greater detail about God's covenant in series to come. However, Matthew chapter 25:31–46 gives us some insight. It is no coincidence that right after the parable of the talents, the Lord Jesus Christ tells us the story of how He will judge the nations. According to this story the business profit is to be used to feed the hungry, nourish the thirsty, house the stranger, clothe the naked, and visit the sick and those who are in prison. I believe that these key areas of focus have both spiritual and natural implications.

> **"The business profit is used to reinvest into the business, enhance your products and services, and fulfill God's covenant."**

"What doth it profit, my brethren, though a man say he hath faith, and have not works? can faith save him? If a brother or sister be naked, and destitute of daily food, and one of you say unto them, Depart in peace, be ye warmed and filled; notwithstanding ye give them not those things which are needful to the body; what doth it profit? Even so faith, if it hath not works, is dead, being alone" (James 2:14-17).

a. **To feed the hungry** – to provide both natural nourishment to those who are without food as well as spiritual nourishment to those lacking the Word of God.
   "And thou shalt not glean thy vineyard, neither shalt thou gather every grape of thy vineyard; thou shalt leave them for the poor and stranger: I am the LORD your God" (Leviticus 19:10).

"Jesus answered, 'It is written: "Man does not live on bread alone." (Deuteronomy 8:3, NKJV), (Luke 4:4, NKJV).

"Then Jesus declared, 'I am the bread of life. He who comes to me will never go hungry, and he who believes in me will never be thirsty" (John 6:35, NKJV).

b. **Nourish the thirsty** – to provide natural water to those without water as well as the spiritual water of the Word of God.

"Jesus answered and said unto her, If thou knewest the gift of God, and who it is that saith to thee, Give me to drink; thou wouldest have asked of him, and he would have given thee living water" (John 4:10).

c. **House the stranger** – to provide physical shelter to those without a home as well as a spiritual shelter in Christ.

"In my Father's house are many mansions: if it were not so, I would have told you. I go to prepare a place for you" (John 14:2).

"Do not forget to entertain strangers, for by so doing some people have entertained angels without knowing it" (Hebrews 13:2, NKJV).

d. **Clothe the naked** – to provide physical clothing to those without them and spiritual clothing in the covering of our sins in the blood of Jesus.

"And he said, I heard thy voice in the garden, and I was afraid, because I was naked; and I hid myself. And he said, Who told thee that thou wast naked? Hast thou eaten of the tree, whereof I commanded thee that thou shouldest not eat?" (Genesis 3:10-11).

"Unto Adam also and to his wife did the LORD God make coats of skins, and clothed them" (Genesis 3:21).

e. **Visit the sick** – to provide physical healing to those who suffer illness and spiritual healing to those who are void of the knowledge of God in Christ Jesus.

"The Spirit of the Lord is upon me, because he hath anointed me to preach the gospel to the poor; he hath sent me to heal the brokenhearted, to preach deliverance to the captives, and recovering of sight to the blind, to set at liberty them that are bruised" (Luke 4:18).

"O LORD my God, I cried unto thee, and thou hast healed me" (Psalm 30:2).

"Who forgiveth all thine iniquities; who healeth all thy diseases" (Psalm 103:3).

f. **Visit those in prison** – to provide physical comfort to those who are in prison and deliverance to those who are spiritually bound.

"And ye shall know the truth, and the truth shall make you free" (John 8:32).

"If the Son therefore shall make you free, ye shall be free indeed" (John 8:36).

5. Talents are given to be traded, and not hidden.

"But he that had received one went and digged in the earth, and hid his lord's money" (Matthew 25:18).

To hide means to keep away from the light or to keep away from purpose. In this context, the ground is symbolic of an unproductive state. It is possible to make an excellent salary or run a business generating great revenues and still have your talents hidden in the ground. The abundance or lack of money or work does not determine whether or not you are operating in purpose. Whenever we operate within the realm of security and comfort, our talents are hidden. Whenever our talents are hidden, we will experience some if not all of the following:

II. A false sense of security
III. Complacency
IV. Stress and anxiety

V. Unfulfillment
VI. Emptiness

> **"You cannot use money or work to measure whether you are in purpose or not."**

When your talents are being traded, you will experience some, if not all, of the following:

I.   Fulfillment
II. Contentment
III. Anticipation
IV. Confidence in Christ
V.   A sense of accomplishment

6. Each of us must render an account for the use of our talents

"After a long time the lord of those servants cometh, and reckoneth with them" (Matthew 25:19).

In Luke 19:11–27 the story of the talents is told by Jesus again, and in this version the master specifically tells his servants, *"Do business till I come."* Our Master, the Lord Jesus Christ is coming back, and upon His return we must be able to render an account to Him of our stewardship over the talents He placed in our care. In the end times Christians will be held accountable both for their spiritual as well as their natural stewardship.

> **"In the end times Christians will be held into account of their spiritual and natural stewardship."**

7. The reward of our stewardship is the increase of our responsibility and the entrance into the joy of the Lord (the ultimate fulfillment).

"His lord said unto him, Well done, thou good and faithful servant: thou hast been faithful over a few things, I will make thee ruler over many things: enter thou into the joy of thy lord" (Matthew 25:21).

Earlier we said that profit is not the reward for the Biblical Entrepreneur. What then is the reward for our good stewardship? Our reward is two-fold: 1) an increase in responsibility and 2) greater fulfillment. In the world system, responsibility is often viewed as a negative rather than a positive. Due to this worldly way of thinking that most of us have grown up with, you are probably wondering, how is increasing my responsibility a reward? Isn't decreasing my level of responsibility the goal?

Permit me to elaborate. Have you ever had a job in which you received a promotion without having produced more work? Have you ever met an entrepreneur whose profit increased without having greater numbers of customers, employees and physical assets? These are both examples of increased responsibility. God is looking for people with whom He can trust His things. Whenever He finds such, the better they handle what they already have, the more He gives them to handle. The good news is that when you operate in purpose and in God's plan for your life, more responsibility will actually be a joy. It is proof that God is pleased with your stewardship. This leads us to the second reward: greater fulfillment. Being profitable with your talents not only increases your responsibility but it will bring you greater fulfillment.

> **"Profit is the increase of responsibility and greater fulfillment."**

8. Each of us will receive equal rewards in spite of the number of talents we start out with.

"He also that had received two talents came and said, Lord, thou deliveredst unto me two talents: behold, I have gained two other talents beside them. His lord said unto him, Well done, good and faithful servant: thou hast been faithful over a few things, I will make thee ruler over many things: enter thou into the joy of thy lord" (Matthew 25:22-23).

God will reward each of us equally, meaning that we will each receive greater responsibility, and greater fulfillment. As stated earlier, comparison is fruitless because talents are given in proportion to the calling on our lives. The reward is the fulfillment, not money or power. Our only concern should be how faithful we are with what we are given, whether little or much. We are to use our talents in proportion to our abilities. Don't worry about the size of your business but rather focus on its productivity. In business terms, rather than focusing on gross revenue, focus on return on investment.

9. **The root cause of poor stewardship over the talents God has given us is often fear.**

"Then he which had received the one talent came and said, Lord, I knew thee that thou art an hard man, reaping where thou hast not sown, and gathering where thou hast not strawed: And I was afraid, and went and hid thy talent in the earth: lo, there thou hast that is thine" (Matthew 25:24-25).

Fear is anxiety caused by real or perceived danger, which can hinder our ability to be productive. Many Christians who struggle with fear are familiar with the acts of God, but are ignorant of His ways. This fact is proven in Scripture with Moses and the children of Israel. The children of Israel knew the acts of God, and hid in their tents when God invited them to come closer. Moses, who knew His ways, went up to the mountain of God, and came away with the Ten Commandments, and the opportunity to speak to God 'face to face.' Those of us who limit ourselves to God's acts tend to manifest the following attributes:

I. Fear
II. Doubt
III. Stress and anxiety
IV. Ungratefulness
V. Greed and selfishness
VI. Playing it safe
VII. Laziness
VIII. Walking by sight and not by faith
IX. Confidence in self
X. Manipulation

Those who know the ways of God tend to:

I. Have reverence for God
II. Trust in the Lord in all their ways
III. Be risk takers
IV. Focus on serving others
V. Be content
VI. Be fulfilled
VII. Walk by faith

> **"Those who act out of fear claim to know God but are only familiar with His acts and not His ways."**

If you study the story of Moses and the children of Israel on their journey from Egypt to the Promised Land you will discover the above listed characteristics. The response that the servant with one talent gave was that, based on his knowledge of the master, he was afraid of what he would do if he lost the talents. Had he really known the master, who represents God, he would have known that He is a God of mercy, justice, forgiveness and compassion who works all things together for our good because we love Him and are *called* according to His purpose. Which God are you familiar with? Have you hesitated to use your talents because of the fear that if you lose them or make mistakes God will punish you? Look at Adam, David, Peter and many others in the

Bible who made mistakes even after experiencing the goodness of God. Though they suffered the consequences of their actions, God forgave and restored them. Never allow fear to cause you to not utilize your talents.

> **"Never allow fear to cause you not to utilize your talents."**

10. Those who hide their talents are considered wicked and slothful.

"His lord answered and said unto him, Thou wicked and slothful servant, thou knewest that I reap where I sowed not, and gather where I have not strawed: Thou oughtest therefore to have put my money to the exchangers, and then at my coming I should have received mine own with usury" (Matthew 25:26-27).

Wicked and slothful--harsh terms; but that is exactly how God views His children who neglect to share their talents, and instead hide them. One of the worst things a child of God can be is selfish, for that is the exact opposite of who God is. God is love, and there is no selfishness in love. When our greatest concern is what is best for us, God considers that wickedness. When we are self-centered, we are acting outside of God's purpose for our lives. Our whole reason for being is to love and serve Him—and how do we do that? By serving others with the gifts He has given us. If all He wanted was for us to give our talents right back to Him, He could have kept them. Similarly, many Christians are so heavenly minded that they fail to live out God's principles while here in the earth. He said, do business until I come.

The business you operate is not solely for your benefit, but it is for the benefit of others. Remember, He gave us power to get wealth so that He could accomplish His covenant. We are instruments through whom God wishes to accomplish His will, and He cannot do that until we get out of our comfort zone and utilize the talents He has provided. Not to do this is to be slothful or lazy. It is a lack of willingness to make any effort.

Work is essential to accomplishing the will of God for our lives. After God created Adam, He gave him work to do. The apostle Paul tells us that if a man does not work he should not eat. I have heard many who desire to become entrepreneurs say they want to start their own business so they no longer have to work hard. That is the wrong reason to start a business. As a matter of fact, I advise those who do not want to work hard to work for someone else rather than start a business. Starting a business will demand more out of you both spiritually and naturally than ever before. However, if it is what God has called you to do, the rewards will be greater than you have ever experienced in your life.

> "Starting a business will demand more out of you spiritually and naturally than you ever had to give in your life."

11. God's economy rewards productivity and punishes unproductivity.

"Take therefore the talent from him, and give it unto him which hath ten talents. And cast ye the unprofitable servant into outer darkness: there shall be weeping and gnashing of teeth" (Matthew 25:28, 30).

Many feel that the marketplace is unfair because it tends to favor the rich and exclude the poor. This is particularly noticeable when comparing minority communities with other communities. We tend to blame this disparity on the seemingly unjust capitalist system. However, capitalism is not the sole instrument responsible for the disparity of wealth in the world. In many cases, though not all, the responsibility lies within certain communities or countries, and their lack of productivity. God is looking for faithful stewards to whom He can entrust His resources. As we have seen in this parable, He moves resources from the control of those who are not productive to the control of those who are. It is our responsibility to be productive and to cause the talents and abilities the Lord has given us to increase in value. What God has purposed for us to have and to manage can only be lost when we exercise poor stewardship over it. God is so concerned about stewardship that He would rather see a non believer being productive with His resources than to leave them in the hands of a believer who is not productive. God is not a wasteful God.

"God is not a wasteful God."

---

12.   God's economy is not fair; it is just.

"For unto every one that hath shall be given, and he shall have abundance: but from him that hath not shall be taken away even that which he hath" (Matthew 25:29).

Most people, including Christians, are concerned about fairness. In God's economy, however, fairness is not relevant. The key is justice. Justice involves that which is in line with God's character, while fairness is that which takes into account human reasoning and influence. Consider the fact that the master took the talent of the servant who only had one and gave it to him who already had ten.

It would appear to me that the servant with one talent was not treated fairly. He didn't lose the talent and did the servant with the ten talents really need more? It seems to me that he had enough. In God's economy, the important thing is the fulfillment of His ultimate plan. Because the person with one talent would not do the job, God moved on to the one who would. It was nothing personal; it was merely business…God's business. No act of God is ever unfair or fair, but just. He cannot be unjust. It was not fair that one man, Jesus would die for the sins of the entire world, but it was just.

"For the kingdom of heaven is like a landowner who went out early in the morning to hire men to work in his vineyard. He agreed to pay them a

denarius for the day and sent them into his vineyard. About the third hour he went out and saw others standing in the marketplace doing nothing. He told them, 'You also go and work in my vineyard, and I will pay you whatever is right.' So they went. He went out again about the sixth hour and the ninth hour and did the same thing. About the eleventh hour he went out and found still others standing around. He asked them, 'Why have you been standing here all day long doing nothing?' 'Because no one has hired us,' they answered. He said to them, 'You also go and work in my vineyard.' When evening came, the owner of the vineyard said to his foreman, 'Call the workers and pay them their wages, beginning with the last ones hired and going on to the first.' The workers who were hired about the eleventh hour came and each received a denarius. So when those came who were hired first, they expected to receive more. But each one of them also received a denarius. When they received it, they began to grumble against the landowner. 'These men who were hired last worked only one hour,' they said, 'and you have made them equal to us who have borne the burden of the work and the heat of the day.' But he answered one of them, 'Friend, I am not being unfair to you. Didn't you agree to work for a denarius? Take your pay and go. I want to give the man who was hired last the same as I gave you. Don't I have the right to do what I want with my own money? Or are you envious because I am generous?' So the last will be first, and the first will be last"
(Matthew 20:1-16, NKJV).

CHAPTER REVIEW

- God has given each of us abilities, gifts, skills and treasures to use profitably for His glory.
- God holds us responsible for our stewardship over those abilities, gifts, skills and treasures we have been given.
- God views us as wicked and slothful when we fail to utilize our talents.
- God's economy is not fair; it is just.

2

What is Biblical Entrepreneurship?

"For the kingdom of heaven is as a man travelling into a far country, who called his own servants, and delivered unto them his goods. And unto one he gave five talents, to another two, and to another one; to every man according to his several ability; and straightway took his journey" (Matthew 25:14).

Biblical Entrepreneurship is a biblically based process of identifying opportunities, taking calculated risks, solving problems, and exercising business stewardship for profit. In Biblical Entrepreneurship, the bible is your guide and everything you do is based on the Word of God. As you identify your opportunity and use your gifts, skills, and treasures to provide goods and services, you must keep your mind focused on the One who has given you those gifts, skills and treasures and called you to be in business.

After you have identified your opportunity, you will take calculated risks by counting the cost of taking advantage of the opportunity you have identified. As well, you will develop a plan to actualize the opportunity. Once you take the calculated risks, you must solve problems. Biblical Entrepreneurship is about solving problems. The opportunity you identify will be a problem that people in your church, community, nation or other parts of the world may have that you can find or develop a product or service to solve. As you solve this and other problems you may encounter, you will be exercising stewardship over a business.

We use the phrase "exercising business stewardship" instead of owning a business because the business does not belong to you; it belongs to the Lord, and you are only a steward over it. The business is the entity that you will be using to produce or purchase the product or service you will be selling. As you exercise business stewardship, you will generate a profit. As we discussed earlier whenever you exercise good stewardship over something, a profit is generated. However, this should not be your sole motivation for going into business. Your primary focus should be to serve people through your products and services. Profit in Biblical Entrepreneurship is the fruit of good stewardship, not the goal. Moreover, Biblical Entrepreneurs profit both spiritually and naturally because the profit is the result of good stewardship and obedience to God's Word.

> **Biblical Entrepreneurship is a biblically based process of identifying opportunities taking calculated risks, exercising business stewardship for biblical profit."**

Other definitions of Biblical Entrepreneurship include:

a. Utilizing our talents to exercise stewardship over the resources of God.

"And God blessed them, and God said unto them, Be fruitful, and multiply, and replenish the earth, and subdue it: and have dominion over the fish of the sea, and over the fowl of the air, and over every living thing that moveth upon the earth" (Genesis 1:28).

" Thou madest him to have dominion over the works of thy hands; thou hast put all things under his feet: All sheep and oxen, yea, and the beasts of the field; The fowl of the air, and the fish of the sea, and whatsoever passeth through the paths of the seas. O LORD our Lord, how excellent is thy name in all the earth!" (Psalm 8:6-8).

b. Utilizing our talents to meet natural needs within the Body of Christ.

"And in those days, when the number of the disciples was multiplied, there arose a murmuring of the Grecians against the Hebrews, because their widows were neglected in the daily ministration. Then the twelve called the multitude of the disciples unto them, and said, It is not reason that we should leave the word of God, and serve tables. Wherefore, brethren, look ye out among you seven men of honest report, full of the Holy Ghost and wisdom, whom we may appoint over this business" (Acts 6:1-3).

"Now there are diversities of gifts, but the same Spirit. And there are differences of administrations, but the same Lord. And there are diversities of operations, but it is the same God which worketh all in all. But the manifestation of the Spirit is given to every man to profit withal" (1 Corinthians12:4-7).

c. Doing business based on the Word of God, and not based on the system of this world nor according to our carnal minds.

"Trust in the LORD with all thine heart; and lean not unto thine own understanding. In all thy ways acknowledge him, and he shall direct thy paths. Happy is the man that findeth wisdom, and the man that getteth understanding. For the merchandise of it is better than the merchandise of silver, and the gain thereof than fine gold. She is more precious than rubies: and all the things thou canst desire are not to be compared unto her." (Proverbs 3:5,13-15).

d. Being a witness for the Lord Jesus Christ in business.

"But ye shall receive power, after that the Holy Ghost is come upon you: and ye shall be witnesses unto me both in Jerusalem, and in all Judaea, and in Samaria, and unto the uttermost part of the earth" (Acts 1:8).

CHAPTER REVIEW

- Biblical Entrepreneurship is a biblically based process of identifying opportunities, taking calculated risks, solving problems, and exercising business stewardship for profit.
- We must utilize our talents to exercise good stewardship over the resources of God and to meet natural needs within the Body of Christ.
- We must do business based upon the Word of God, and not the ways of the world.
- We are witnesses for the Lord Jesus Christ in business.

3

Biblical Entrepreneurship Principles

"Therefore whoever hears these sayings of mine, and does them, I will liken him to a wise man who built his house on the rock: and the rain descended, the floods came, and the winds blew and beat on that house; and it did not fall, for it was founded on the rock" (Matthew 7:24,25, NKJV)

According to the American Heritage Dictionary (AHD), a principle is a basic truth or law. It is also defined as a rule or law concerning the functioning of a natural or spiritual phenomenon. Jesus teaches us that if we will follow His words, which are principles of success, we will be like a wise man who built his house on a rock. Biblical Entrepreneurship principles allow you to build your business on the rock, the rock of Jesus Christ! Knowing and applying Biblical Entrepreneurship principles effectively will give you an advantage in starting and operating a successful business.

In order for the two servants in the story of the talents to increase their talents, they had to apply principles. They not only had to recognize economic principles, but they also had to apply entrepreneurship principles. One of the benefits of the Biblical Entrepreneurship principles we are going to cover in this chapter is that they are not affected by changes in culture or environment. Therefore, you can use them regardless of your skills, gifts, or business type. These principles can even be applied in ministry or in your place of employment. Whether you are starting a business or not, we encourage you to use these principles, because every born-again believer has been given gifts, skills and treasures by the Lord Jesus and He expects us to be profitable with them. These principles will guide you through the ups and downs of the business, and the changes and shifts of the marketplace.

> **"Knowing and applying Biblical Entrepreneurship principles effectively will give you an advantage in starting and operating a successful business."**

I. Identifying Opportunities

The principle of Identifying Opportunities is recognizing when the timing of God meets preparation. This principle helps to identify God's timing for getting into business or starting a particular business. It also requires you to know your gifts, skills, and treasures, and cooperate with God in developing them, so that you may be prepared when an opportunity comes your way. Moreover, in identifying an opportunity you must be able to recognize beneficial gain in the midst of unfavorable circumstances. Whenever the timing of God meets preparation, an opportunity presents itself. In the following chapters we will take a closer look at the life of Joseph, who, because he cooperated with God and developed his skills, gifts, and treasures was prepared for the opportunity that he was presented with.

II. Taking Calculated Risks

The principle of Taking Calculated Risks is counting all costs to ensure you have sufficient resources to finish. This principle helps you reduce your risk of failure and ensures that you are spiritually, naturally, mentally and emotionally prepared to successfully start and operate a successful business.

"For which of you, intending to build a tower, sitteth not down first, and counteth the cost, whether he have sufficient to finish it?" (Luke 14:28).

III. Solving Problems

The principle of Solving Problems is coming in agreement with the Word of God and therein finding the solution for any situation that presents a need, uncertainty or difficulty. This principle will enable you to keep the challenges of operating a business from stealing your peace. No matter the circumstances, you can find the answer in the Word of God. You may not be able to identify an immediate solution, but you can always receive an immediate peace, if you believe.

"Be careful for nothing; but in every thing by prayer and supplication with thanksgiving let your requests be made known unto God. And the peace of God, which passeth all understanding, shall keep your hearts and minds through Christ Jesus" (Philippians 4:6-7).

IV. Business Stewardship

The principle of Business Stewardship is taking dominion over the natural resources of God in order to serve others, while making a profit for the Kingdom of God. This principle helps you recognize the fact that you own nothing. All that you have (the gifts, skills, treasure, business ideas, and the business) belongs to the Lord Jesus Christ. We are only temporary stewards of His goods.

"O LORD our Lord, how excellent is thy name in all the earth! Who has set thy glory above the heavens. Out of the mouth of babes and sucklings hast thou ordained strength because of thine enemies, that thou mightest still the enemy and the avenger. When I consider thy heavens, the work of thy fingers, the moon and the stars, which thou has ordained; What is man, that thou art mindful of him? And the son of man, that thou visitest him? For thou hast made him a little lower than the angels, and hast crowned him with glory and honour. Thou madest him to have dominion over the works of thy hands; thou hast put all things under his feet: All sheep and oxen, yea, and the beasts of the field; The fowl of the air, and the fish of the sea, and whatsoever passeth through the paths of the seas. O Lord our Lord, how excellent is thy name in all the earth!" (Psalm 8).

V. Biblical Profit

The principle of Biblical Profit is the spiritual and natural gain remaining after all costs are deducted from a business transaction or from the total income of the business. As a Biblical Entrepreneur, you must profit spiritually by obeying the Word of God and naturally by exercising proper stewardship over the business. Just as it does not glorify God when you do not make a profit, it also does not glorify Him when you make a profit at the expense of disobeying His commandments.

"But godliness with contentment is great gain" (I Timothy 6:6).

CHAPTER REVIEW

- A principle is a basic truth or law.
- The five Biblical Entrepreneurship principles are:
  1. Identifying Opportunities
  2. Taking Calculated Risks
  3. Solving Problems
  4. Business Stewardship
  5. Biblical Profit

4

The Difference Between Biblical and Worldly Entrepreneurship

"Envy thou not the oppressor, and choose none of his ways" (Proverbs 3:31).

Though the bible instructs us that we should not envy the oppressor, nor choose any of his ways, many Christian businesspersons fail or become victims to the wiles of the enemy because they have not been obedient to this Scripture. To envy is to have a feeling of discontentment and resentment aroused by desiring someone else's possessions or qualities, accompanied by a strong desire to have them for oneself (AHD).

In the context of this teaching, the oppressor is a non-believer or a believer who is not operating according to the will of God; this person may be in a superior position and tends to use their influence or resources in ways that do not glorify the Lord. Why, you may ask, would someone envy another whose values are obviously contrary to their own, or who is operating contrary to the Word of God? The benefits from taking shortcuts and operating in an unscrupulous manner in business can be tempting; oftentimes, the neighborhood drug dealer is envied because of his car, clothes, money and influence. Sadly, this temptation affects many Christians. They find themselves envying even those who operate contrary to biblical values because they become enamored with their material wealth.

People caught up in "keeping up with the Joneses" ignore the fact that an oppressor employs ungodly means (ways) to acquire the things they possess. What we often fail to realize is that as long as we desire the things the oppressor has, we will end up choosing his ways, and that is essentially what this Scripture is saying: if you envy the oppressor you will choose his ways.

Some of the ways of the oppressor include lying, cheating, intimidation, and other behaviors that we will discuss in more detail. The key to not choosing the ways of the oppressor is to stop lusting after the benefits of the oppressor. Yes, get your focus off of the luxury car and home, money, clothes, and influence. Now, of course we need transportation and we need clothing and we need money to purchase them. And what is wrong with influence, you may ask? Nothing, inherently...but did not the Lord Himself say in Matthew 6:33, that He knows that we have need of things? He also said seek ye first the kingdom and his righteousness and all these things will be added unto you.

Our Lord also said in Psalms 37:4, "if you delight yourself in him he will give you the desires of your heart". In Proverbs 16:8 and 23:4, we are admonished that "better is a little with righteousness than great revenue without right" and "to labor not to be rich". In other words, if you are going to be a Biblical Entrepreneur, you must commit in your heart that unless you can operate a profitable business based on the Word of God and His principles, you will not be in business. You will not seek to succeed in business by any means necessary, but rather, you will obey God by any means necessary. Therefore, you will reject the benefits of the oppressor and seek the benefits of God which do not preclude natural provision, but expand beyond that to include peace of mind and fulfillment. Let's now compare and contrast secular entrepreneurship with Biblical Entrepreneurship.

> **"Some Christians tend to envy others who are operating contrary to their values because of what they have"**

The world sees entrepreneurship as a means for individuals to participate in the free market economy for the purpose of controlling resources and creating wealth for themselves. This limited view of entrepreneurship is what has created today's business environment. This environment uses God's resources and principles for the sake of gain without acknowledging Him. There is little respect or appreciation for the environment; it is often abused and destroyed by businesses for the sake of profit. Employees are often underpaid and laid off at the expense of cheap labor and shareholders' equity. Unfriendly competition is the norm, creating hostility among businesses selling similar products and services. God's laws and even government regulations are often violated for the sake of profit. Products and services are offered by businesses regardless of their moral or ethical value, as long as there is a demand in the marketplace and profits can be made. Accumulating wealth is the name of the game, which often cultivates greed among entrepreneurs, shareholders and business executives.

> **"The world sees entrepreneurship as a means for individuals to participate in the free market economy for the purpose of creating wealth for themselves and controlling resources."**

Consumers are abused by overpriced products and products of low or mediocre quality. The worldly approach to entrepreneurship has caused many God fearing people to stay away from business altogether, or to conclude that business is a worldly practice and those who believe in the Lord Jesus Christ cannot participate in it without compromising their faith. The problem with this conclusion is that it leaves the resources of God and the Christian consumer at the mercy of greedy capitalist. It hinders our ability to be a witness in the market place, it is another example of 'hiding' our talents, and it is contrary to Jesus' statement that we are to be in the world but not of the world. In reality, the problem is not that business is inherently evil; the problem is that most Christians do not realize that God does provide in His word a way for His people to do business.

> "The worldly approach to entrepreneurship has caused many God fearing people to stay away from business, concluding that business is a worldly practice and those who believe in the Lord Jesus Christ cannot participate in it with out compromising their faith."

Entrepreneurship God's way, or Biblical Entrepreneurship, is about exercising stewardship over God's resources to serve others for the benefit of the Kingdom of God. Biblical Entrepreneurship recognizes the Lordship of Jesus Christ over all things and uses business as a means to build His Kingdom through service. Biblical Entrepreneurship recognizes that who you are in church is who you must be while conducting your business affairs. You cannot separate your faith from your business.

Listed below are some key differences between Biblical Entrepreneurship and worldly entrepreneurship.

BIBLICAL ENTREPRENEURSHIP	WORLDLY ENTREPRENEURSHIP
1. Uses spiritual gifts and skills	1. Uses only natural skills
2. Business steward	2. Business owner
3. Biblical profit	3. Worldly profit
4. Ideas inspired by God	4. Self-motivated
5. Directed by the Holy Spirit	5. Self-driven
6. Confidence in God	6. Confidence in self
7. Motivated by love	7. Motivated by money
8. Interdependent	8. Independent
9. Cooperative	9. Competitive
10. Calling	10. Career

11. Kingdom focus	11. Big business focus
12. Enjoys serving others	12. Enjoys commanding others
13. Follows God's methods	13. Originates own methods

When business is operated improperly using worldly ways and methods, the outcome is ultimately the following:

- Death
- The works of the flesh are manifested
- Lack of peace
- Lack of fulfillment
- Temporary rewards
- Others suffer lack
- Eternal punishment

But when business is operated properly using biblical principles, we can experience the following outcomes:

- Abundant life
- The fruit of the Spirit is manifested
- Contentment
- Fulfillment
- Temporal and eternal rewards
- None suffer lack
- The Great Commission is fulfilled

CHAPTER REVIEW

- Christians must not envy others' success, especially the success of the ungodly.
- Secular entrepreneurship is primarily concerned with individual profit: it allows persons to participate in the free market economy for the purpose of creating wealth for themselves and controlling resources.
- Biblical Entrepreneurship allows Christians to exercise stewardship over God's resources to serve others for the benefit of the Kingdom of God.
- Biblical Entrepreneurship requires that we not separate our faith from our businesses.

5

Joseph, an Example of a Biblical Entrepreneur from the Bible

"Now therefore let Pharaoh look out a man discreet and wise, and set him over the land of Egypt" (Genesis 41:33).

<u>A profile of the life of Joseph</u>

Genesis 39-50 profiles the life of a man named Joseph, the eleventh son of an entrepreneur named Jacob, a young dreamer and a man destined for greatness. Jacob's sons were trained to care for his sheep from an early age. Jacob favored Joseph over his other sons, and the fact that Joseph brought a bad report about his brothers to his father increased the jealousy and anger they held toward him. One day, Joseph had a dream which he shared with his brothers; in his dream he saw that he would rule over his brothers and have dominion over them. Then he had another dream and this time shared it not only with his brothers but with his father as well. In this dream, everyone including his father and mother bowed down to him. This dream caused his father to rebuke him and his brothers to hate him even more. Their rage culminated in their throwing him into a pit in an attempt to kill him. However, when they were persuaded that selling him into slavery would be more profitable then killing him they sold him to Midianite traders for twenty pieces of silver.

Joseph was then taken to Egypt, where he was sold to Potiphar, an officer of the ruling Pharaoh. While working as Potiphar's slave the Lord prospered everything he did. His good conduct and success soon earned him the highest position in Potiphar's household. Later Potiphar's wife became infatuated with Joseph and made several attempts to commit adultery with him. When he refused, she accused him of sexual harassment and Joseph was sent to prison. While in prison, Joseph's behavior earned him a position of authority over the other prisoners. Pharaoh's butler and baker were among the prisoners Joseph met. Each of these men had a dream, which Joseph interpreted. Joseph asked the butler (whose dream was favorable), to remember him when Pharaoh released him from prison. When the butler left prison, he forgot about Joseph, and Joseph spent more years in prison.

One day when Pharaoh had a dream that neither his magicians nor the wise men of Egypt could interpret, the butler remembered Joseph and mentioned him to Pharaoh. Joseph was then called to appear before Pharaoh. When Pharaoh told Joseph that he had heard that Joseph was the only one who could interpret his dream, Joseph's response was, "Not I but God will give Pharaoh an answer of peace" (Gen 41:16). He correctly interpreted Pharaoh's dreams, predicting seven years of plenty and seven years of famine. Joseph also advised Pharaoh to appoint someone to store up food during the plentiful years before the famine came. To Joseph's surprise, Pharaoh appointed him as governor and second only to Pharaoh himself in Egypt. This was a position of great prestige. Under Joseph's stewardship, much food was reserved and the land prospered. Joseph was rewarded with a wife, with servants, and with the respect of all in the land.

When the famine struck, Joseph had already successfully harvested enough food. People from surrounding lands, including those from Joseph's homeland of Canaan, came to him to buy food. These people included Joseph's own family. When Joseph's brothers came to buy food from Egypt, only Benjamin, Joseph's only brother of same mother and father, did not come. Jacob kept him back in Canaan for fear some harm would befall him, as it had Joseph. When his brothers came to Egypt, they bowed down before Joseph with their faces to the earth, seeking food to sustain their family. Joseph recognized his brothers, but they did not recognize him. He remembered the dream which he had dreamed about them in his youth. Joseph treated them roughly, acting as though they were spies who had come to Egypt to investigate the land.

The brothers did all they could to explain that they were not spies, but all sons of one man and were originally twelve but one died. They went on to say that the youngest was left behind with their father, and they had truly come to buy food because of the famine. However, Joseph continued to treat them roughly and even put them in prison as a test. He demanded that they bring their younger brother to Egypt to prove their innocence, and ordered one of his brothers, Simeon, held in prison until the rest returned with the youngest brother. At different times during their interaction, Joseph would turn from his brothers and weep. As Joseph prepared to send the brothers back to Canaan, without their knowledge, he commanded that their bags be filled with food, their money restored, and that they be given food for the road.

When they returned to Jacob they shared the story with him, but Jacob did not believe them. He also refused to let Benjamin go back with them in fear that he would lose him as he did Joseph and Simeon who had been placed in prison. Once the food they had brought from Egypt ran out, Jacob had no choice but to ask them to go back to Egypt to get more food and reluctantly sent Benjamin with them at the insistence of another son, Judah. He sent them with a basket of fruit as a present for the governor of Egypt (Joseph) and twice the money they needed so they could return the money that was put into their bags.

When they arrived in Egypt and Joseph saw Benjamin he prepared a feast for them at his home. They were sent ahead to Joseph's house and were given excellent treatment. When Joseph arrived, they gave him the present they brought for him. He inquired about their father Jacob, greeted Benjamin, and because he yearned for his brother, he went to his room alone to weep. Then he washed his face and came out of the room to eat with them. Benjamin was given five times more than everyone else. As they prepared to return to Canaan, Joseph commanded the stewards of his house to fill the men's bags with food, as much as they could carry and to put their money back in their bags. He also asked that they put a silver cup in the bag of the youngest, Benjamin.

Once they left for Canaan, while they were on the road Joseph sent one of his stewards to go confront the brothers about having stolen his silver cup but they denied it. He had the steward search their belongings; whoever was found in possession of the cup would become Joseph's slave. The cup was found in Benjamin's bag. Judah requested that he keep all of them as his slaves, but Joseph said no. He said he would only keep the one in whose bag the cup was found because the rest were innocent and they could return to Canaan. Judah then pleaded with Joseph to take him instead as his slave and release Benjamin with the rest of his brothers. His father was an old man, and would die if he lost his youngest son, and Judah had promised that he would bring him back, or bear the blame forever.

At that point, Joseph could no longer restrain himself and he asked all of the Egyptians to leave the room. Only his brothers remained. Joseph then revealed himself to his brothers and wept aloud. He said to his brothers, *"I am Joseph your brother, whom you sold into Egypt! But now, do not therefore be grieved or angry with yourselves because you sold me here; for God sent me before you to preserve life"* (Gen 45:4-5, NKJV). He then made arrangements for his brothers to bring his father back with them and for all of them to settle in Egypt under his care.

Joseph not only successfully prepared Egypt for the time of famine, he also successfully managed its resources during that time, all the while being used by God to ensure the welfare of the children of Israel. Let us look at how God prepared Joseph to fulfill this great task.

Joseph's Wilderness: How God prepared him to fulfill his ultimate destiny

Though Joseph was destined by God for greatness, he was not born ready for greatness; he displayed youthful arrogance, was spoiled by his father and very naïve.

These traits are demonstrated by these key facts:

a. He brought a bad report to his father about his brothers
b. He was his father's favorite
c. He boasted to his brothers and father about his dream in which he would rule over them and they would serve him

"These are the generations of Jacob. Joseph, being seventeen years old, was feeding the flock with his brethren; and the lad was with the sons of Bilhah, and with the sons of Zilpah, his father's wives: and Joseph brought unto his father their evil report. Now Israel loved Joseph more than all his children, because he was the son of his old age: and he made him a coat of many colours" (Genesis 37:2-3).

"And Joseph dreamed a dream, and he told it his brethren: and they hated him yet the more. And he said unto them, Hear, I pray you, this dream which I have dreamed: For, behold, we were binding sheaves in the field, and, lo, my sheaf arose, and also stood upright; and, behold, your sheaves stood round about, and made obeisance to my sheaf. And his brethren said to him, Shalt thou indeed reign over us? or shalt thou indeed have dominion over us? And they hated him yet the more for his dreams, and for his words. And he dreamed yet another dream, and told it his brethren, and said, Behold, I have dreamed a dream more; and, behold, the sun and the moon and the eleven stars made obeisance to me. And he told it to his father, and to his brethren: and his father rebuked him, and said unto him, What is this dream that thou hast dreamed? Shall I and thy mother and thy brethren indeed come to bow down ourselves to thee to the earth?" (Genesis 37:5-10).

Because of this lack of readiness and maturity to walk in his divine calling, the Lord had to prepare and mature Joseph for his destiny. He had to go through what I call the *wilderness experience*. The wilderness experience is a combination of trials, tests and temptations allowed by God to perfect us and to enable us to fulfill His will for our lives. Most of us believe we are ready the minute we receive the vision, especially if it is clear in our minds. However, the next several years will most likely be full of lessons to prepare us for our ultimate destiny. Since God works through human vessels and natural circumstances, He used the jealousy and envy of his brothers to send Joseph through a process of trials and tests that would prepare him for his calling. Through this wilderness, he experienced four major trials and tests, along with several other temptations in between:

The first trial he experienced was the pit - The pit is a hopeless state where only God's mercy can bring you through. The pit was designed to humble him. In the pit, he had no one to lean on or call upon but God; he felt he would surely die--only to be removed and sent into slavery. The pit is that season of time when the circumstances we experience can cause hopelessness. During the pit experience he had to pray and believe God for a miracle. If God hadn't intervened he would have died. God often intervenes in strange ways. He was rescued from death—but went from the pit into slavery, a better situation but still challenging. During the pit experience, he learned that man shall not live by bread alone but by every word that proceeds out of the mouth of God.

"And when they saw him afar off, even before he came near unto them, they conspired against him to slay him. And they said one to another, Behold, this dreamer cometh. Come now therefore, and let us slay him, and cast him into some pit, and we will say, some evil beast hath devoured him: and we shall see what will become of his dreams. And Reuben heard it, and he delivered him out of their hands; and said, Let us not kill him. And Reuben said unto them, Shed no blood, but cast him into this pit that is in the wilderness, and lay no hand upon him; that he might rid him out of their hands, to deliver him to his father again. And it came to pass, when Joseph was come unto his brethren, that they stripped Joseph out of his coat, his coat of many colours that was on him; And they took him, and cast him into a pit: and the pit was empty, there was no water in it. And they sat down to eat bread: and they lifted up their eyes and looked, and, behold, a company of Ishmeelites came from Gilead with their camels bearing spicery and balm and myrrh, going to carry it down to Egypt. And Judah said unto his brethren, What profit is it if we slay our brother, and conceal his blood? Come, and let us sell him to the Ishmeelites, and let not our hand be upon him; for he is our brother and our flesh. And his brethren were content. Then there passed by Midianites merchantmen; and they drew and lifted up Joseph out of the pit, and sold Joseph to the Ishmeelites for twenty pieces

of silver: and they brought Joseph into Egypt. And the Midianites sold him into Egypt unto Potiphar, an officer of Pharaoh's, and captain of the guard" (Genesis 37:19-28, 36).

The second trial and test was slavery - Slavery was designed to teach him how to be a good steward over natural resources and to learn the ways of the Egyptian ruling class, among whom he would live and work later on. He served well as Potiphar's steward and hoped that it would eventually lead to his freedom, but he was tempted by Potiphar's wife who made sexual advances towards him several times. From these incidents, Joseph also learned to flee temptation, to respect his employer, and to never make a choice for his own benefit, that exalted itself against the knowledge of God.

"And Joseph was brought down to Egypt; and Potiphar, an officer of Pharaoh, captain of the guard, an Egyptian, bought him of the hands of the Ishmeelites, which had brought him down thither. And the LORD was with Joseph, and he was a prosperous man; and he was in the house of his master the Egyptian. And his master saw that the LORD was with him, and that the LORD made all that he did to prosper in his hand. And Joseph found grace in his sight, and he served him: and he made him overseer over his house, and all that he had he put into his hand. And it came to pass from the time that he had made him overseer in his house, and over all that he had, that the LORD blessed the Egyptian's house for Joseph's sake; and the blessing of the LORD was upon all that he had in the house, and in the field. And he left all that he had in Joseph's hand; and he knew not aught he had, save the bread which he did eat.

And Joseph was a goodly person, and well favoured. And it came to pass after these things, that his master's wife cast her eyes upon Joseph; and she said, Lie with me. But he refused, and said unto his master's wife, Behold, my master wotteth not what is with me in the house, and he hath committed all that he hath to my hand; There is none greater in this house than I; neither hath he kept back any thing from me but thee, because thou art his wife: how then can I do this great wickedness, and sin against God? And it came to pass, as she spake to Joseph day by day that he hearkened not unto her, to lie by her, or to be with her. And it came to pass about this time, that

41

Joseph went into the house to do his business; and there was none of the men of the house there within. And she caught him by his garment, saying, Lie with me: and he left his garment in her hand, and fled, and got him out.

And it came to pass, when she saw that he had left his garment in her hand, and was fled forth, That she called unto the men of her house, and spake unto them, saying, See, he hath brought in an Hebrew unto us to mock us; he came in unto me to lie with me, and I cried with a loud voice: And it came to pass, when he heard that I lifted up my voice and cried, that he left his garment with me, and fled, and got him out. And she laid up his garment by her, until his lord came home. And she spake unto him according to these words, saying, The Hebrew servant, which thou hast brought unto us, came in unto me to mock me: And it came to pass, as I lifted up my voice and cried, that he left his garment with me, and fled out. And it came to pass, when his master heard the words of his wife, which she spake unto him, saying, After this manner did thy servant to me; that his wrath was kindled" (Genesis 39:1-19).

The third trial was prison - Prison is the transitional period between the wilderness and ultimate greatness. Since prison was the gateway to his destiny, the Lord orchestrated that he would be imprisoned in the same place where the king's prisoners were confined. Prison taught him leadership. While in prison the Lord prospered him and he was put in charge of all the prisoners. This allowed him to learn the leadership skills he would need to be governor over Egypt.

"And Joseph's master took him, and put him into the prison, a place where the king's prisoners were bound: and he was there in the prison. But the LORD was with Joseph, and shewed him mercy, and gave him favour in the sight of the keeper of the prison. And the keeper of the prison committed to Joseph's hand all the prisoners that were in the prison; and whatsoever they did there, he was the doer of it. The keeper of the prison looked not to any thing that was under his hand; because the LORD was with him, and that which he did, the LORD made it to prosper" (Genesis 39:20-23).

Finally, Joseph was tested through confrontation – The confrontation occurred when he faced the people that were responsible for selling him into slavery. Once elevated as governor of Egypt, Joseph faced his brothers as they came to Egypt to buy food for their family in Canaan. As a result of this test, Joseph learned forgiveness and was healed from the hurts and pains from the wilderness years. He had to forgive those the Lord used to perfect him. If he had not forgiven them, his destiny could not have been revealed to him, and thus he could not walk in it.

"Now when Jacob saw that there was corn in Egypt, Jacob said unto his sons, Why do ye look one upon another? And he said, Behold, I have heard that there is corn in Egypt: get you down thither, and buy for us from thence; that we may live, and not die. And Joseph's ten brethren went down to buy corn in Egypt. But Benjamin, Joseph's brother, Jacob sent not with his brethren; for he said, Lest peradventure mischief befall him. And the sons of Israel came to buy corn among those that came: for the famine was in the land of Canaan.

And Joseph was the governor over the land, and he it was that sold to all the people of the land: and Joseph's brethren came, and bowed down themselves before him with their faces to the earth. And Joseph saw his brethren, and he knew them, but made himself strange unto them, and spake roughly unto them; and he said unto them, Whence come ye? And they said, From the land of Canaan to buy food. And Joseph knew his brethren, but they knew not him. And Joseph remembered the dreams which he dreamed of them, and said unto them, Ye are spies; to see the nakedness of the land ye are come. Then Joseph could not refrain himself before all them that stood by him; and he cried, Cause every man to go out from me. And there stood no man with him, while Joseph made himself known unto his brethren. And Joseph said unto his brethren, Come near to me, I pray you. And they came near. And he said, I am Joseph your brother, whom ye sold into Egypt. Now therefore be not grieved, nor angry with yourselves, that ye sold me hither: for God did send me before you to preserve life.(Genesis 42:1-9, 45:1, 4).

Joseph's destiny is revealed

When Joseph had his dream as a teenager, his interpretation was that he would rule over his brothers and parents and they would serve him. Joseph's immaturity caused him to define greatness as a position of lordship versus one of service -- a lesson Jesus would later teach His disciples in Mark 10:35-45:

"But Jesus called them to him, and saith unto them, Ye know that they which are accounted to rule over the Gentiles exercise lordship over them; and their great ones exercise authority upon them. But so shall it not be among you: but whosoever will be great among you, shall be your minister: And whosoever of you will be the chiefest, shall be servant of all. For even the Son of man came not to be ministered unto, but to minister, and to give his life a ransom for many" (Mark 10:42:45).

This attitude led to the need for the Lord to take him through the wilderness experience. Once Joseph was fully perfected the Lord revealed his ultimate destiny to him which was not one of lordship over his brothers but one of service towards them. What allowed Joseph to see his destiny was the fact that he forgave his brothers. Prior to the forgiveness he was attempting to ensure his well-being as well as the well-being of his younger brother Benjamin. However, once he forgave, he realized that it was not just about him and his brother but about his entire family; even those who sold him into slavery.

Though Joseph saw himself as the center of the story, it was really never about him, but his brothers. More specifically, it was about Judah. Why Judah, you may ask? From the loins of Judah would come our Lord and Savior Jesus Christ. The Lord sent Joseph ahead to Egypt because he knew there was a famine coming and he needed to protect the Seed; that Seed that would take away the sins of the entire human race so that whoever would believe in him would not perish but have everlasting life (John 3:16). It was about protecting Jesus Christ our Savior. We can even see Christ manifested in Judah when he interceded on behalf of Benjamin, putting his own life on the line that Benjamin would be saved. That act foreshadowed what was to come as Christ would come and lay down His life so that we might be saved. In that act it was not Judah who was speaking but Christ Himself.

"And Judah said, What shall we say unto my lord? what shall we speak? or how shall we clear ourselves? God hath found out the iniquity of thy servants: behold, we are my lord's servants, both we, and he also with whom the cup is found. And he said, God forbid that I should do so: but the man in whose hand the cup is found, he shall be my servant; and as for you, get you up in peace unto your father.

Then Judah came near unto him, and said, Oh my lord, let thy servant, I pray thee, speak a word in my lord's ears, and let not thine anger burn against thy servant: for thou art even as Pharaoh. My lord asked his servants, saying, Have ye a father, or a brother? And we said unto my lord, We have a father, an old man, and a child of his old age, a little one; and his brother is dead, and he alone is left of his mother, and his father loveth him. And thou saidst unto thy servants, Bring him down unto me, that I may set mine eyes upon him. And we said unto my lord, The lad cannot leave his father: for if he should leave his father, his father would die. And thou saidst unto thy servants, Except your youngest brother come down with you, ye shall see my face no more.

And it came to pass when we came up unto thy servant my father, we told him the words of my lord. And our father said, Go again, and buy us a little food. And we said, We cannot go down: if our youngest brother be with us, then will we go down: for we may not see the man's face, except our youngest brother be with us. And thy servant my father said unto us, Ye know that my wife bare me two sons: And the one went out from me, and I said, Surely he is torn in pieces; and I saw him not since: And if ye take this also from me, and mischief befall him, ye shall bring down my gray hairs with sorrow to the grave. Now therefore when I come to thy servant my father, and the lad be not with us; seeing that his life is bound up in the lad's life; It shall come to pass, when he seeth that the lad is not with us, that he will die: and thy servants shall bring down the gray hairs of thy servant our father with sorrow to the grave. For thy servant became surety for the lad unto my father, saying, If I bring him not unto thee, then I shall bear the blame to my father for ever. Now therefore, I pray thee, let thy servant abide instead of the lad a bondman to my lord; and let the lad go up with his brethren. For how shall I go up to my father, and the lad be not with me? lest peradventure I see the evil that shall come on my father" (Genesis 44:16-34).

How Joseph used the five BE principles to resolve the famine in Egypt

1. Identifying Opportunities

Though Joseph was sold into slavery, the Lord used many circumstances and experiences to prepare him for the time he would be steward over Egypt. Joseph was sold into slavery to Potiphar which gave him the experience he needed to be a steward over food and household goods. Joseph gained leadership experience while in prison. The prison keeper promoted him to a leadership position. To ensure that he would be prepared for the prestigious position of governor over Egypt, Joseph's character and faithfulness were tested while he was a steward in Potiphar's house and as head of the prisoners in the King's prison. Joseph saw the faithfulness of God in his life, which gave him the courage to give the credit to God before Pharaoh (who was viewed by the Egyptians as a god-like figure), at the risk of his own life. Joseph's experiences humbled him and enabled God to exalt him in due time.

Like Joseph, God has allowed you to go through many circumstances and experiences, some positive and some negative. Keep in mind that these experiences are preparing you for opportunities that God will set before you. According to Romans 8:28, *"And we know that all things work together for good to those who love God, to those who are called according to his purpose."* Be assured and know if you love God and remain in His will for your life, he will work all things out together for your good because you are called according to His purpose. Since you are reading this book it is possible that you are doing so because you want to make sure you please Him as you start and operate your business. Although you may be unsure of the purpose for which God is preparing you, be faithful and diligent in all of your responsibilities such as your job, ministry or business. These are the ways God prepares His leaders. Whenever something negative happens to you, through no fault of your own, or due to your own poor choices, determine to see it as a way that God is preparing you for an opportunity to serve Him and His people in the future.

2. Taking Calculated Risks

From Joseph's childhood, we can see that he was a risk taker. He took the risk of sharing his dream with his brothers, which unfortunately made them jealous of him, and resulted in them selling him into slavery. While serving as the steward over Potiphar's house, Joseph took the risk of refusing to cooperate with the desires of Potiphar's wife. He chose rather to honor the trust of his master and his God. He also took another risk by inquiring about the well-being of the baker and the butler and volunteering to interpret their dreams. These acts of courage, the confidence in his destiny and total reliance on Jehovah God prepared Joseph for the ultimate calculated risk of his life. This in turn led him out of prison and established him as governor over Egypt.

Joseph was given the responsibility of preparing Egypt for the time of famine. The bible does not address the effort Joseph invested in planning this project, but there is enough evidence for us to know that he did not just go around gathering food for seven years. Joseph had to determine where to store the food, how much to store, and where to get the food. He also had to determine who would help him acquire and distribute the food, and how much doing so would cost. Moreover, he had to determine how the food would be paid for and how much money he would charge for the food during the time of famine. This required him to develop a plan. Another great risk that Joseph took was when he chose to rise above his hurt, fears and anger over his brothers' betrayal and reveal himself to them. This brought about forgiveness which led to the revelation of his ultimate destiny.

Once you identify your opportunity, there is always a risk that you must take to take advantage of that opportunity. The risk may be as small as the possibility of losing a few hundred dollars from your personal savings to as big as the possibility of losing millions of dollars you borrowed from investors or the bank. Your challenge will be to take the time to count all your costs and plan before acting on whatever you want to do. Though business is about risk taking, successful business people are not those who take a lot of risks but those who minimize their risks. Risks are minimized through proper planning and preparation.

3. Problem Solving

Joseph was a problem solver. This is evident by his experiences in prison. For example, he helped the butler and the baker solve their problems without even being asked. This problem-solving mindset must have been what continued to give him favor regardless of his circumstances. Joseph also successfully interpreted Pharaoh's dream and resolved the problem of famine in Egypt. Much like Joseph, problem solvers do not stop working until the problem is resolved. They have a positive attitude, rely on the Lord for their solutions and know there is always a solution for whatever problem is placed before them. They have confidence in the words of Jesus in Matthew 19:26 *"With men this is impossible; but with God all things are possible."* As you prepare to start your business or grow your existing business, maintain a problem-solving attitude. Know that whatever problems you may face, God has already prepared a solution for you. Do not allow any problem to overwhelm you, and do not give up until God has revealed to you His answer. While the answer tarries stay in the peace of God -- the peace that surpasses your understanding.

4. Business Stewardship

Prayerfully, it is clear how Joseph can be an example of a Biblical Entrepreneur though he did not own a business. Remember, Biblical Entrepreneurship is not about ownership but rather stewardship and service. Joseph owned nothing but he was a steward over the resources in Egypt. Joseph also lacked nothing because Pharaoh provided for all of his needs. Not only that, but he was also able to be a blessing to his family when they joined him in Egypt. As you operate your business, remember that you own nothing and that God is the owner of everything, even the profit you will make in the business. In Haggai 2:8, God's Word reads, *"The silver is mine, and the gold is mine, saith the Lord of hosts."* However, just like Joseph, as you exercise good stewardship over God's resources through business, He will provide for you. A good steward never suffers lack but always has enough to meet his needs and to be a blessing to others.

5. Biblical Profit

During the time of famine, Joseph opened the barn and made food available to the people of Egypt and the surrounding nations. Joseph could have felt sorry for the people and given the food away for free, but that would not have been good stewardship. He charged a reasonable price for the food. When the people ran out of currency (money), Joseph found a way for them to still have access to the food without compromising his stewardship. All the while he remained focused on serving the people and not just on making money, as a true Biblical Entrepreneur would do. Joseph gave the people the option of bartering with him. Bartering is an exchange between two or more parties that does not require money, but both parties receive something of similar value. It is also the exchange of goods or services *for* other goods or services of equal value. As a Biblical Entrepreneur, your business must make a profit because God is glorified when his stewards make a profit. The key, however, is to remember that you cannot profit at the expense of the people. Since you are there to serve them, you must always try to find ways to serve them -- without losing money. Also key is to ensure that your customers appreciate your product or service, *for where there is no investment, there is no appreciation* (Episcopal Pastor John A. Cherry, FTHCM). Conversely, if your services are not appreciated, there will be no investment.

Joseph successfully prepared Egypt for the time of famine and managed its resources during the time of famine, enabling God to use him to ensure the welfare of the children of Israel.

Lessons we can learn from the life of Joseph

Like Joseph, most entrepreneurs are individuals destined for greatness but not born prepared for it. They are dreamers, oftentimes with an unrealistic view of themselves. Many are arrogant, prideful and feel as though they are the center of the universe. Their motive for being in business is usually self-centered, based on an internal drive for independence. A common theme for many entrepreneurs is, "I want to start a business so that I can be my own boss." They do not realize that starting a business does not make you a boss but rather a servant. As an entrepreneur you are God's steward, called to serve customers and your employees. Though many Christian entrepreneurs will profess to believe this and even practice it, the wilderness experience allows them to see if they really mean what they say.

"And you shall remember that the Lord your God led you all the way these forty years in the wilderness, to humble you and test you, to know what was in your heart, whether you would keep His commandments or not." (Deuteronomy 8:2, NKJV).

All born again believers who are called of God to carry out a great work must go through the wilderness. You have either gone through your wilderness, are going through it now or you will go through it in the future. However, like Joseph, the wilderness is designed to perfect you, not to destroy you. It is designed to bring you into a state of total dependency upon God so that He may exalt you and reveal to you the fullness of your destiny. Therefore, do not disdain the trials and tests you are going through, will go through or have gone through. Look at what lessons you can learn from them that will enable you to fulfill God's plan for your life.

"He humbled you, causing you to hunger and then feeding you with manna, which neither you nor your fathers had known, to teach you that man does not live on bread alone but on every word that comes from the mouth of the LORD. Your clothes did not wear out and your feet did not swell during these forty years. Know then in your heart that as a man disciplines his son, so the LORD your God disciplines you." (Deuteronomy 8:3-5)

Our ultimate destiny is not our business or the job we have; those are mere instruments that God uses to enable us to fulfill our destiny. Our destiny rests in how we are using whatever God has blessed us with to conform to His image and likeness and to be a witness for Him in the marketplace. The results should be that more souls come to know Jesus Christ as their personal Lord and Savior through our personal witness and our ministry. I don't believe the Lord is really concerned with the type of business you start or even if you start one. He is concerned with whether or not you have used the talents that He placed under your care profitably, because His instructions are "do business until I come," for He is coming back.

"But remember the LORD your God, for it is he who gives you the ability to produce wealth, and so confirms his covenant, which he swore to your forefathers, as it is today" (Deuteronomy 8:18, NIV).

CHAPTER REVIEW

- God will use a "wilderness" time to prepare us for our ultimate destiny.
- The four phases of Joseph's wilderness trials and test were the pit, slavery, prison and confrontation.
- Joseph identified opportunities while he was in the midst of his wilderness.
- Joseph was a calculated risk taker who was able to rise from slavery to the second-highest position in the land.
- Joseph was a problem solver who resolved the problem of famine in Egypt.
- Joseph owned nothing but was a steward over all the resources of Egypt.
- Joseph made a profit for the Pharaoh, even in the midst of a famine.
- The Lord desires that we utilize what He has given us, profitably, and that we "do business" until He comes again.

Workbook Exercises

Answer the following questions as discussed in the chapters:

1. Read Matthew 25:14-30 and explain the story in your own words.

_____

_____

_____

_____

_____

_____

2. List the five Biblical Entrepreneurship principles.

_____

_____

_____

_____

3. List five negative consequences of the worldly approach to entrepreneurship.

_____

_____

_____

_____

_____

_____

4. Can believers in the Lord Jesus Christ conduct business without compromising their faith? Why or why not?

----

5. What is the problem with the view that business cannot be done God's way?

----

6. Match the following BE characteristics with the appropriate worldly characteristics by placing a number next to the words in the worldly column that corresponds to the appropriate biblical characteristics.

Biblical	Worldly
1. Uses spiritual gifts and skills	__Confidence in self
2. Business steward	__Enjoys commanding others
3. Biblical profit	__Career
4. Ideas inspired by God	__Competitive
5. Directed by the Holy Spirit	__Originates own method

6. Confidence in God   __Independent
7. Motivated by love   __Self-motivated
7. Interdependent   __Business owner
9. Cooperative   __Self-driven
10. Calling   __Uses only natural skills
11. Kingdom focus   __Worldly profit
12. Enjoys serving others   __Motivated by money
13. Follows God's methods   __Big business focus

7. What was Joseph's mandate when he was released from prison?

_____

_____

_____

_____

8. How did Joseph use the five Biblical Entrepreneurship principles while in Egypt?

_____

_____

_____

_____

_____

_____

9. Why did Joseph's brothers sell him into slavery?

_____

_____

_____

10. Why was Joseph imprisoned?

_____

_____

_____

_____

11. What caused Joseph to prosper in Potiphar's house and in prison?

_____

_____

_____

_____

12. Why was Joseph released from prison?

_____

_____

_____

_____

13. Was Joseph right when he bartered with the people instead of giving them the food for free after they ran out of currency? What business lessons can we learn from this?

_____

_____

_____

_____

I. BE Vocabulary
Define each word listed below.

1. Ability:

_____

_____

_____

2. Skill:

_____

_____

_____

3. Biblical Entrepreneurship:

_____

_____

_____

4. Talents:

_____

_____

_____

5. Principle:

_____

_____

_____

6. Identifying Opportunities:

_____

_____

_____

7. Taking Calculated Risks:

_____

_____

_____

8. Solving Problems:

_____

_____

_____

9. Business Stewardship:

_____

_____

_____

10. Biblical Profit:

_____

_____

_____

11. Worldly entrepreneurship:

_____

_____

_____

12. Currency:

_____

_____

_____

13. Bartering:

_____

_____

_____

14. Treasure:

_____

_____

_____

II. BE Sentences
Fill in the appropriate words in the following sentences.

1. The master gave his servant talents according to their_____

   _____.

2. As a Biblical Entrepreneur, the _____ is your guide to everything you do.

3. To be a successful Biblical Entrepreneur, you must know biblical _____ and ensure their proper application in starting and operating a business.

4. _____, _____ recognizes the Lordship of Jesus Christ in all things.

5. You cannot separate your faith from your _____ _____.

6. Joseph's experience in Egypt _____him and allowed God to exalt him in due time.

7. Though business is about taking a risk, successful Biblical Entrepreneurs are not those who take lots of risks but those who _____ their _____.

8. _____ _____ do not stop working until the _____ is solved.

9. BE is not about _____ownership but _____ _____ and _____.

10. A good _____steward never suffers lack but always has sufficient resources to meet his needs and be a blessing to others.

11. Joseph could have felt sorry for the people and given the food away for _____ but that would have been bad _____ _____.

12. Where there is no _____ there is no _____.

13. You cannot _____ at the expense of the people you are called to serve.

III. Biblical Entrepreneurship Scriptures

Fill in the blank with the appropriate word (s).

1. His lord said unto him, _____-_____, thou _____ _____ and _____ servant: thou hast been faithful over a _____ things, I will make thee _____ over many things: enter thou into the _____ of thy lord. He also that had received two talents came and said, Lord, thou deliverest unto me two talents: behold, I have _____ two other talents beside them **(Matthew 25:21).**

2. Then he which had received the _____ talent came and said, Lord, I knew thee that thou art an _____ man, reaping where thou hast not sown, and gathering where thou hast not strawed: And I was _____, and went and _____ thy talent in the _____: lo, there thou hast that is thine. His lord answered and said unto him, Thou _____ and _____ servant, thou knewest that I _____ where I _____ not, and _____ _____ where I have not _____: Thou oughtest therefore to have put my _____ to the _____ _____, and *then* at my coming I should have received mine own with _____. Take therefore the _____ _____ from him, and give *it* unto him which hath ____ _____ talents. For unto every one that _____ shall be _____, and he shall have _____: but from him that hath _____ shall be _____ -_____ even that which he _____. And cast ye the _____ servant into outer darkness: there shall be weeping and gnashing of teeth **(Matthew 25:24-30).**

3. Envy thou not the _____, and choose none of his _____ (Proverbs 3:31).

4. And we know that _____ things work _____ for _____ to them that _____ God, to them who are the _____ according to his _____ ____ **(Romans 8:28).**

5. But Jesus beheld them, and said unto them, With men this is _____; but with God all things are _____ _____ **(Matthew 19:26).**

6. The _____ *is* mine, and the _____ *is* mine, saith the LORD of hosts **(Haggai 2:8).**

V. BE Business Application

1. Reflect upon your own life, have you had a wilderness experience? What was it? What did you learn from it? How did God use it to humble you and perfect you to fulfill His purpose and plan for your life?

_____

_____

_____

_____

_____

_____

_____

_____

_____

_____

_____

_____

_____

_____

2. Identify a company that is using a biblical approach to entrepreneurship. Explain what the company does and how it is impacting society in a positive way.

----

3. Identify a company that is using a worldly approach to entrepreneurship. Explain what the company does and how it is impacting society in a negative way.

----

4. Other than Joseph, select another person in the bible who you believe exemplifies Biblical Entrepreneurship? Explain why you selected them.

A special note from the Author

Thank your for taking the time to read this first book of the Biblical Entrepreneurship Marketplace Series. I hope and pray that it has blessed you and helped you to assess your talents and utilize them profitably to the glory and honor of the Lord Jesus Christ.

The next book in this series will be titled "The Three Essential Ingredients to Entrepreneurship Success". These ingredients are attitude, character and goal setting. We will define attitude and character and their significance to doing business God's way. We will discuss the characteristics that make up the attitude and character of a Biblical entrepreneur, how to develop these characteristics and the rewards that comes with having a Biblical Entrepreneurship attitude. We will also discuss how to set and achieve goals based on our responsibilities. We will conclude with a profile of another Biblical Entrepreneur, Brother Tyrone Grigsby, the Christian business man responsible for bringing me to Christ. We will look at the childhood experiences that shaped his views in business, how he came to know Christ, what inspired him to contribute to the development of Biblical Entrepreneurship, and how he was able to build a $50 million company, which he later sold and is now valued at several billion dollars. Until then, please pray that the Lord continues to give us the inspiration, the grace, and the favor to help others fulfill God's plan for their lives through business.

Glossary

Ability – the power and strength granted by God that enables us to use our gifts, skills and treasures to His glory

Assets – something of value that can be used to generate a profit

Bartering – an exchange between two or more parties that does not require money, but both parties receive something of similar value

Biblical Entrepreneurship – a biblically based process of identifying opportunities, taking calculated risks, solving problems and exercising business stewardship for profit

Biblical Profit – the spiritual and natural gain remaining after all costs are deducted from a business transaction or from the total income of the business

Business Stewardship – taking dominion over the natural resources of God to serve others while making a profit for the Kingdom of God

Currency - money

Gifts – God's spiritual blessings upon believers, by the operation of the Holy Spirit, to fulfill a divine purpose

Identifying Opportunities – recognizing when the timing of God meets preparation

Principle – a basic truth or law; a rule or law concerning the functioning of a natural or spiritual phenomenon

Skill – a God-given, natural trade, technique, or special expertise requiring the use of the hand, body or mind

Solving Problems – coming in agreement with the Word of God and finding the solution for a situation that presents a need, uncertainty or difficulty

Taking Calculated Risks – counting all costs to ensure adequate resources to finish

Talents – also known as assets

Treasures – wealth in the form of valuables or money

Worldly entrepreneurship – a means for individuals to participate in the free market economy for the purpose of controlling resources and creating wealth for themselves

ABOUT THE NEHEMIAH PROJECT INTERNATIONAL MINISTRIES (NPIM)

Inspired by the Lord Jesus Christ, the Nehemiah Project International Ministries (NPIM) was founded in 1999 by Patrice and Gina Tsague. The purpose of NPIM is to use entrepreneurship as a tool to empower the body of Christ and lead the lost to a saving knowledge of Jesus Christ.   NPIM Inc. is an international non-profit 501© 3 Christian entrepreneurship training and business support service organization whose **mission is to help people fulfill God's plan for their lives through business.**

NPIM works in partnership with churches, ministries, businesses and Christian educational institutions in the United States and in other parts of the world to equip Christian adults and teens with the knowledge of how to start and operate a business based on the Word of God. NPIM also coordinates local and overseas outreach activities such as mission tours, conferences, and television and radio programs and financially supports overseas missions. To date NPIM has developed a proprietary business discipleship curriculum called "Biblical Entrepreneurship," established an affiliate chapter in Central Africa Cameroon called Nehemiah Project Cameroon (NPC) which is completely staffed by Cameroonians. NPC trains local individuals and business owners how to start and operate a business or to enhance their existing business based on biblical principles. NPIM also has an online campus that delivers the Biblical Entrepreneurship training courses throughout the world. We also provide business support services to our alumnus and other Christian businesses through our business coaching program and the BE Alumni association. NPIM is an affiliate ministry of Bethel World Outreach International Ministries Inc.

Programs and Services
- BE Resources
  - -Principles of Biblical Entrepreneurship
  - -Practices of Biblical Entrepreneurship
  - -Biblical Entrepreneurship Planning Guide

- Training
    - BE I
    - BE II
    - BE III
  -Biblical Entrepreneurship Course for Youth
  -BE Workshops, Conferences and Retreats
  -Other Training
    - BE for Couples
    - BE Financial Stewardship
- Business Support
  -Alumni Services
    - Alumni Association
    - Alumni Directory
  -Weekly BE Devotional
  -Business Coaching
- Outreach
  -CKW Legacy Fund
  BE Support Fund

For more information about any of our programs and services please visit our website or contact us at:

Phone: 703-916-1180
Email: ptsague@nehemiahproject.org
1940 Duke Street Suite 200
Alexandria VA 22314
www.nehemiahproject.org

Nehemiah Publishing Order Form

Ship To:
Name:_____
Address:_____
_____
H Phone: _____
Business#: _____
Cell: _____
Email:_____

Bill To: (If Different than Ship to)
Name:_____
Address:_____
_____
H Phone: _____
Business#: _____
Cell: _____
Email:_____

Payment Method: Cash ○ Check ○ #_____ Money Order ○
Select Credit Card: VISA ○ MC ○ American Express ○ Discovery ○
Credit card number: _____ **Exp Date:** _____

Description	Qty	Amount	Total
Principles of Biblical Entrepreneurship Workbook		$35.00	
Practices of Biblical Entrepreneurship Workbook		$35.00	
Biblical Entrepreneurship Planning Guide		$35.00	
What Is Biblical Entrepreneurship Part I—Tape Series		$35.00	
Workbook and Tape Series		$60.00	
Individual Tapes—1 & 2 - Introducing Biblical Entrepreneurship - I		$5.00	
Individual Tapes—3 & 4 - Introducing Biblical Entrepreneurship II		$5.00	
Individual Tapes— 5 & 6 - Identifying Opportunities		$5.00	
Individual Tapes— 7 & 8 - Taking Calculated Risk		$5.00	
Individual Tapes— 9 & 10 - Solving Problems		$5.00	
Individual Tapes— 11 &12 - Business Stewardship		$5.00	
Individual Tapes— 13 &14 - Biblical Profit		$5.00	
RBTW Video		$35.00	
RBTW DVD		$40.00	
Shipping: Single Tapes, add $2.00			
Tape Series and Books add $5.00			
		Total	

Make checks payable to: Nehemiah Publishing   **Phone:** 703-916-1180,

Mail to: 10715 Brink Rd., Germantown, MD 20876
Email: gtsague@nehemiahproject.org

About the Author

Patrice Tsague is a servant of the Lord Jesus Christ, husband of Gina and father of two Gabrielle and Danielle. He is burdened by the need to see the body of Christ equipped with the knowledge of Biblical Entrepreneurship, which he uses as a tool to lead the lost to Christ. Patrice Tsague has years of experience as a Biblical Entrepreneurship Certified Instructor and as a Business Coach/Consultant to a number of small to medium sized businesses. He currently serves as the Chief Servant Officer of the Nehemiah Project International Ministries, and Nehemiah Publishing. Patrice Tsague's educational experience includes college courses from Montgomery College, bible and ministerial courses from the School of Knowledge at From the Heart Church Ministries, Entrepreneurship Instructor Certification from the National Foundation for Teaching Entrepreneurship and the National Foundation for Teaching Economics. Most of his business knowledge has been acquired through hands on experience, founding and running the Nehemiah Project International Ministries, watching his mother establish and run numerous business ventures, mentors, self study and guidance from the Holy Spirit. Patrice is an active member of Bethel World Outreach Church Ministries where he serves as Special Assistant to Bishop Darlingston Johnson.

Printed in the United States
90736LV00003B/268-291/A